BAROQUE ART

ART HISTORY BOOK FOR CHILDREN

Children's Arts, Music & Photography Books

Speedy Publishing LLC
40 E. Main St. #1156
Newark, DE 19711
www.speedypublishing.com

In this book, we're going to talk about Baroque Art. So, let's get right to it!

WHAT IS BAROQUE ART?

The term Baroque is used to describe a particular style of art that was dominant in the 1600s to 1700s. Paintings and sculpture were influenced by this style. Architecture and music were also shaped by the characteristics of Baroque Art.

Baroque Angel - St. Johns co-Cathedral. Valletta, Malta

Martin Luther posting his 95 Theses in 1517.

THE ORIGIN OF BAROQUE ART

In 1517, Martin Luther, who was originally a Catholic priest, wrote a manuscript called the 95 Theses. In this document, he criticized the Catholic Church for the way they were receiving payments for allowing people into heaven. These indulgences were corrupt and Luther was asking the Church to reform. His criticisms eventually led to the development of new Protestant denominations.

The Catholic Church was very powerful, and the leaders were concerned that these new religions would damage their strength. This attempt to combat the influence of the Reformation was called the ***"Counter-Reformation."*** Pope Paul III convened the Council of Trent in 1545 so that the Church could solidify its position. The Church didn't back down on its doctrine.

Portrait Pope Paul III Farnese

owever, it did take steps to reform the internal corruption that Martin Luther had criticized. This reform and critical self-examination actually strengthened the Church, even though it didn't stop other religious denominations from forming.

Ceiling Fresco by Pierre de Cortone, Palazzo Barberini.

So, what does this event have to do with Baroque Art? Even though the printing press was starting to spread across Europe, most people in European countries were not yet educated. Many people still couldn't read. The Church wanted the people to truly understand the beauty and power of the religion they professed.

Church Sant'Andrea della Valle, Piazza Vidoni, built in Baroque style, 1608 AD. Rome, Italy.

They wanted religious art to communicate this with emotion, so that people would be inspired to hold fast with their beliefs and continue to worship at their local Catholic churches.

Interiors and architectural details of Saint Louis des Francais church, in Rome, Italy

S ome of the new Protestants, such as the Calvinists, believed that churches should be plain and simple with no elaborate artwork. The Catholic Church disagreed with this philosophy and said that artwork should reflect the glory and grandeur of God. These expressions of faith became Baroque Art.

The Inspiration of Saint Matthew by Caravaggio.

This form of art took the realism and action shown in Renaissance art and added more drama, power, and raw emotion to it. It was designed to inspire in the viewer a desire for greater piety and devotion to God and the Catholic religion.

The Calling of Saint Matthew by Caravaggio.

CHARACTERISTICS OF BAROQUE ART

Baroque Art is easy to identify because it has lots of distinct characteristics. Here are some of the common features of Baroque Art.

- It's very high contrast, which means that the light stands out against the dark and shadows.

- It has lots of overlapping of figures and elements, as opposed to Renaissance Art where figures and objects were in defined planes.

Supper at Emmaus by Caravaggio.

- It contains very dramatic use of different colors, when color is used.

- It uses elaborate settings and decorations.

- It includes images that are dramatic and straightforward.

- It attempts to make the viewer a participant in the scene.

- Its scenes appear real, both psychologically and physically.

- It contains lots of movement and action as well as sweeping physical gestures.

The Triumph of the Immaculate.

THEMES OF BAROQUE ART

In addition to these common characteristics, Baroque Art has common themes. The themes are frequently a meeting between the divine and the human, such as spiritual visions, sudden conversions, intense divine ecstasy, the exact moment of death or martyrdom, events that are psychologically gripping, and rays of bright light that have divine significance.

St Nicholas Church at Old Town Square in Prague.

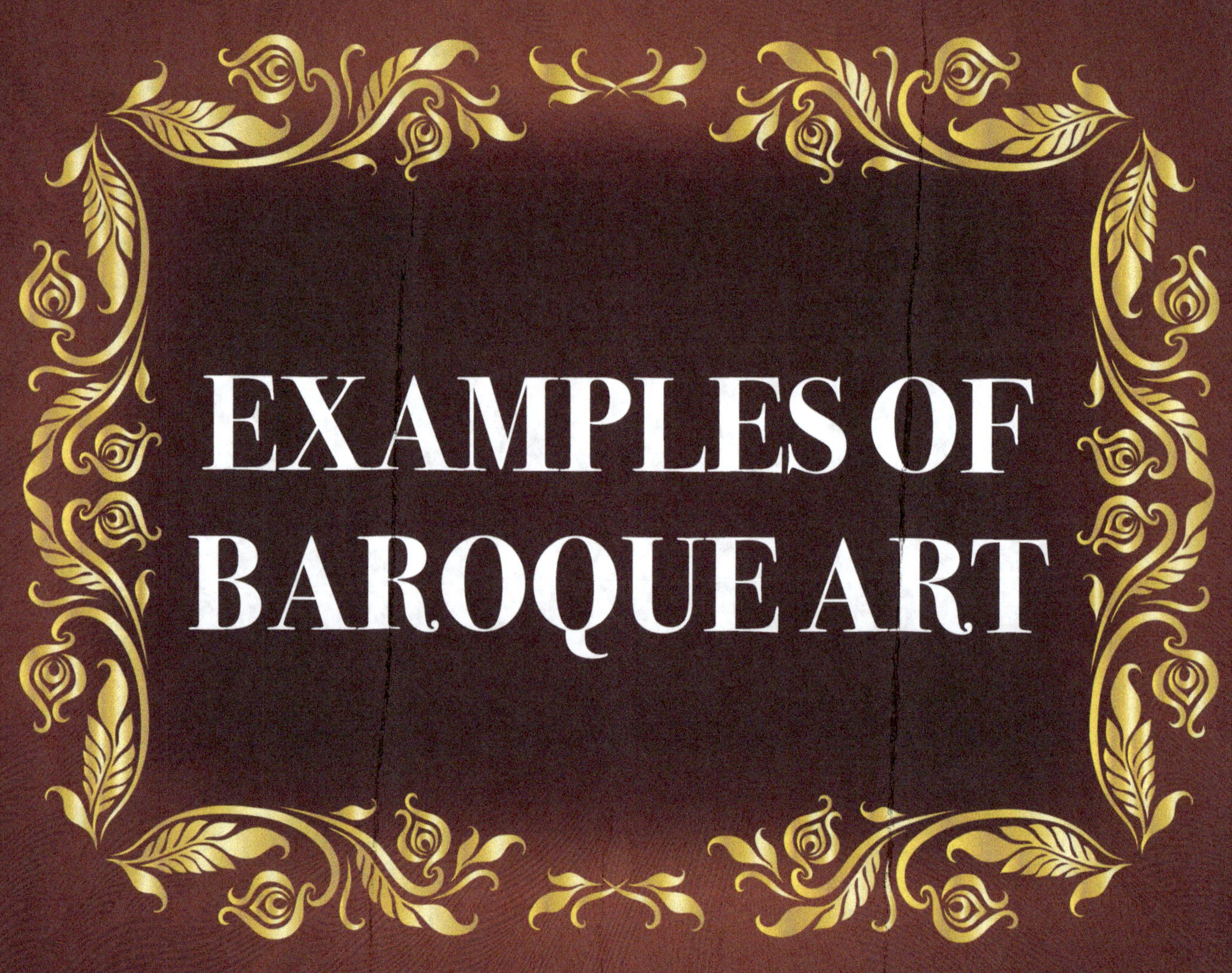

EXAMPLES OF BAROQUE ART

Interior of the Basilica of
Sant 'Andrea della Valle

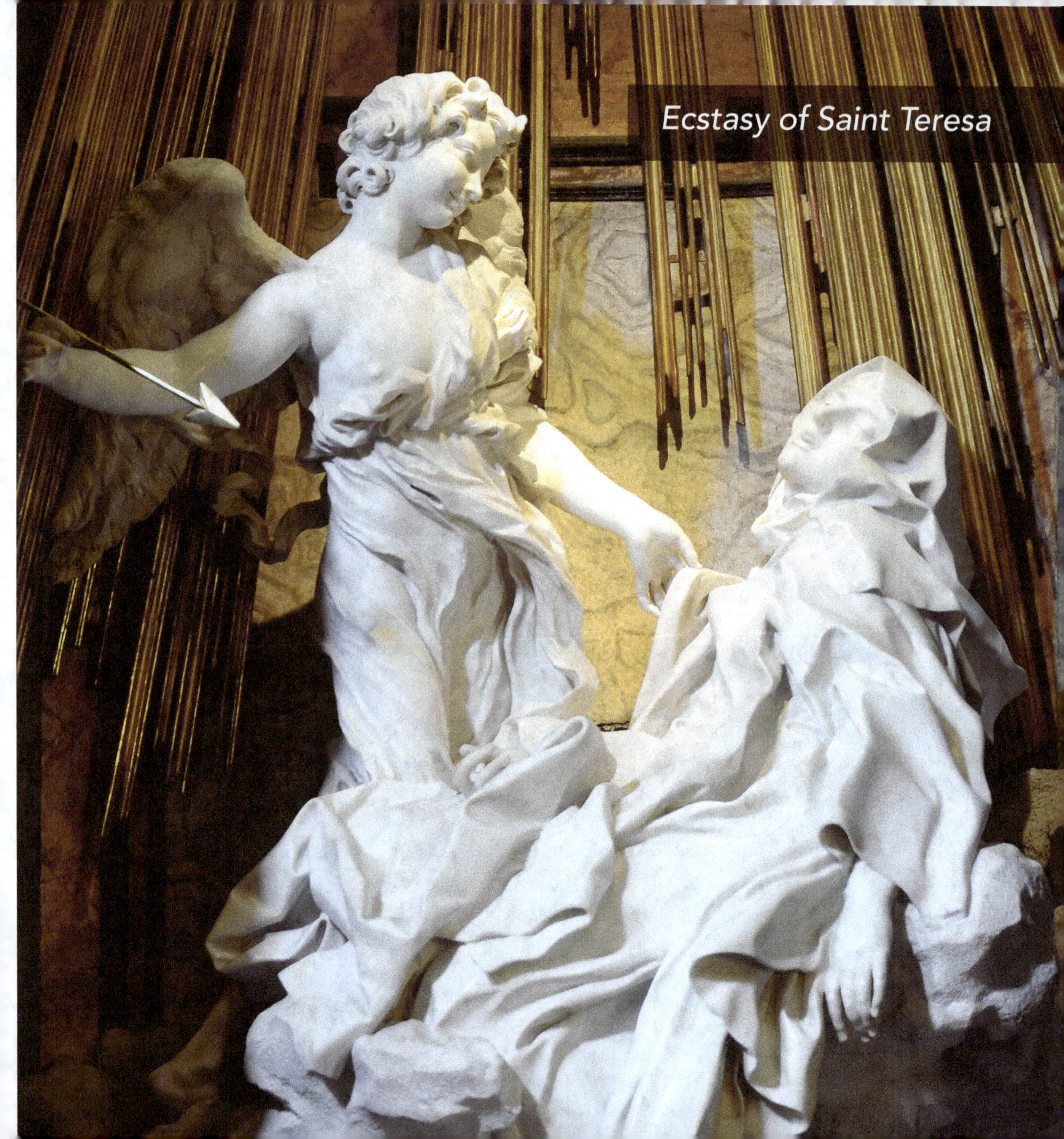
Ecstasy of Saint Teresa

The Ecstasy of Saint Teresa
by Gian Lorenzo Bernini

This beautiful sculpture created in 1652 is an example of a moment in time when the divine came down upon the Earth. A nun who had visions, Saint Teresa had a mystical experience. An angel came down and pierced her with an arrow. The scene in the sculpture is the moment before this happens. The arrow held divine love and even though the pain Saint Teresa experienced was excruciating, it brought her into spiritual ecstasy.

This scene has drama and the wooden pieces behind the painting highlight the sculpture with rays of light. The light streams in from a hidden window above, making the sculpture intensely lit.

Portrait of Gian Lorenzo Bernini

The Conversion on the Way to Damascas
by Caravaggio

This Baroque masterpiece painted by Caravaggio in 1601 shows the moment when Saul, soon to be St. Paul, is struck down off his horse by God's intense light. Once again, the theme of this painting is the sudden entrance of the divine into the realm of Earth. The intense play of light and dark emphasizes the meaning in this painting.

Conversion on the way to Damascus by Caravaggio

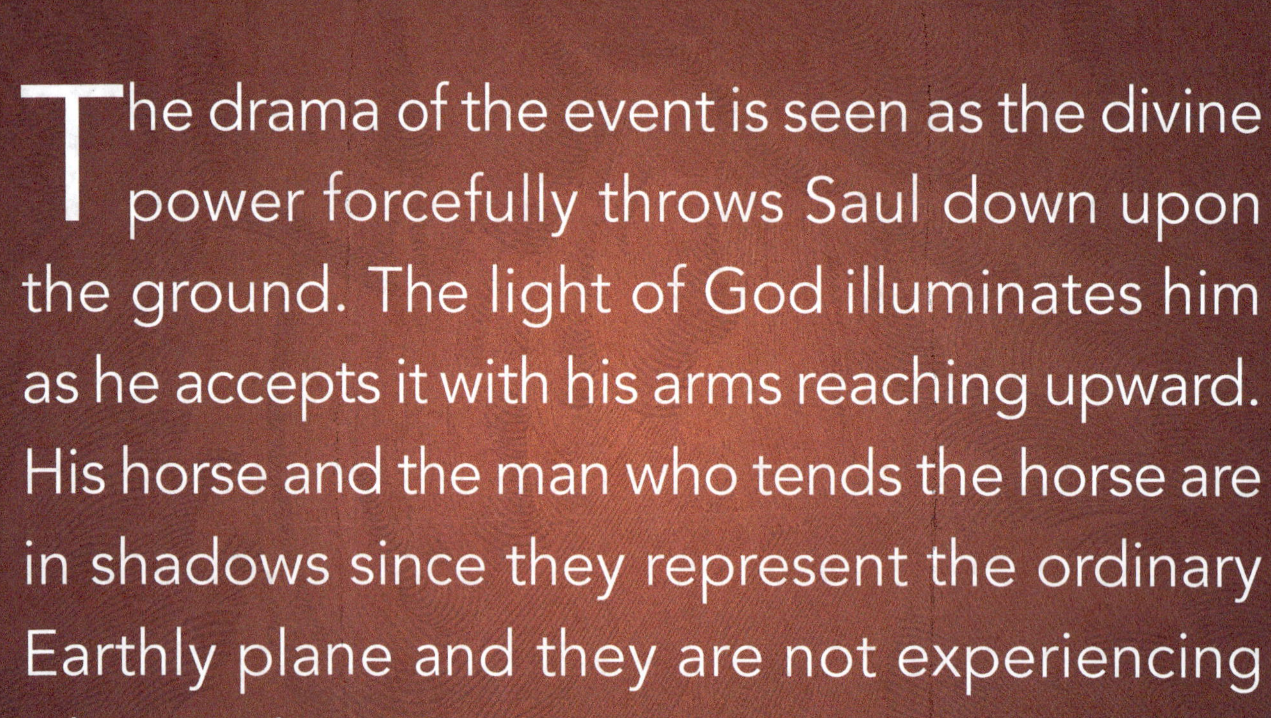

The drama of the event is seen as the divine power forcefully throws Saul down upon the ground. The light of God illuminates him as he accepts it with his arms reaching upward. His horse and the man who tends the horse are in shadows since they represent the ordinary Earthly plane and they are not experiencing what Saul is experiencing.

Portrait of Michelangelo Merisi da Caravaggio

The Crucifixion of Saint Peter
by Caravaggio

Caravaggio's paintings were very realistic. In contrast to paintings from the Renaissance that showed some realism, Caravaggio's paintings were raw and unsentimental in their portrayal. Sometimes viewers found them objectionable because the scenes shown were so effective that viewers actually felt the suffering the figures in the painting were feeling.

Crucifixion of Saint Peter by Caravaggio.

In this painting from 1601, Caravaggio has used dramatic lighting to show three Roman soldiers as they try to lift St. Peter on his cross. St. Peter asked that he be hung upside down because he didn't feel he was worthy to die in the

same way Christ had died. The light of God shines on Peter and the Romans attempting to lift him are in the shadows to signify the crime they are committing by killing St. Peter.

The Four Continents by Peter Paul Rubens

The Four Continents
by Peter Paul Rubens

Rubens was a leading painter in the Counter-Reformation movement. This painting, which he painted in 1615, is a combination of history, mythology, and religion. It has many of the typical characteristics of Baroque Art. It has vivid colors and overlapping figures. It has stark contrast between light and shadow. Each of the four continents, Europe, Asia, America, and Africa, are represented by a different woman.

The men in the painting represent the major rivers of each continent. There are many elements in the painting that make it appear more like a mythological painting from the Renaissance. The painting was meant to represent the spread of the Catholic religion throughout the world. Rubens painted women with soft, plump forms and today we use the word "rubenesque" to describe women with this type of shape.

Study of a River God by Peter Paul Rubens

Descent from the Cross
by Rembrandt

Rembrandt is known for his portrait paintings, but he also painted masterful landscapes as well as paintings with religious themes. In this painting, which he created in 1634, the moment when Christ is taken down from the cross is depicted. Once again, the Baroque themes can be seen in the overlapping figures and the dramatic use of light and shadow.

Descent from the Cross by Rembrandt van Rijn

Christ's body and the women who faithfully remained with him are lit, and the other figures are in darkness. The shroud where he will soon return to life is lit as well. Rembrandt worked toward a composition that displayed the "greatest and yet most natural movement" within his paintings.

Another series of Rembrandt's paintings where you can see the dramatic play of light and shadow is the philosopher series: ***Philosopher in Meditation, Philosopher with an Open Book,*** and ***Philosopher Reading.*** Although the philosophers are shown at a distance in these paintings, the viewer is invited to quietly enter these rooms and participate in the philosophers' thoughts.

Philosopher in Meditation by Rembrandt

Triumph of St. Ignatius of Loyola
by Andrea Pozzo

Pozzo began this masterpiece of Baroque Art in 1685. It is a fresco that is a ceiling painting in the Church of St. Ignatius. The ceiling was completely flat, but a viewer looking at the painting is instead seeing a dome shape. It looks as if the walls and ceiling are reaching toward an opening to the sky and the realms of heaven.

Triumph of St. Ignatius of Loyola by Andrea Pozzo.

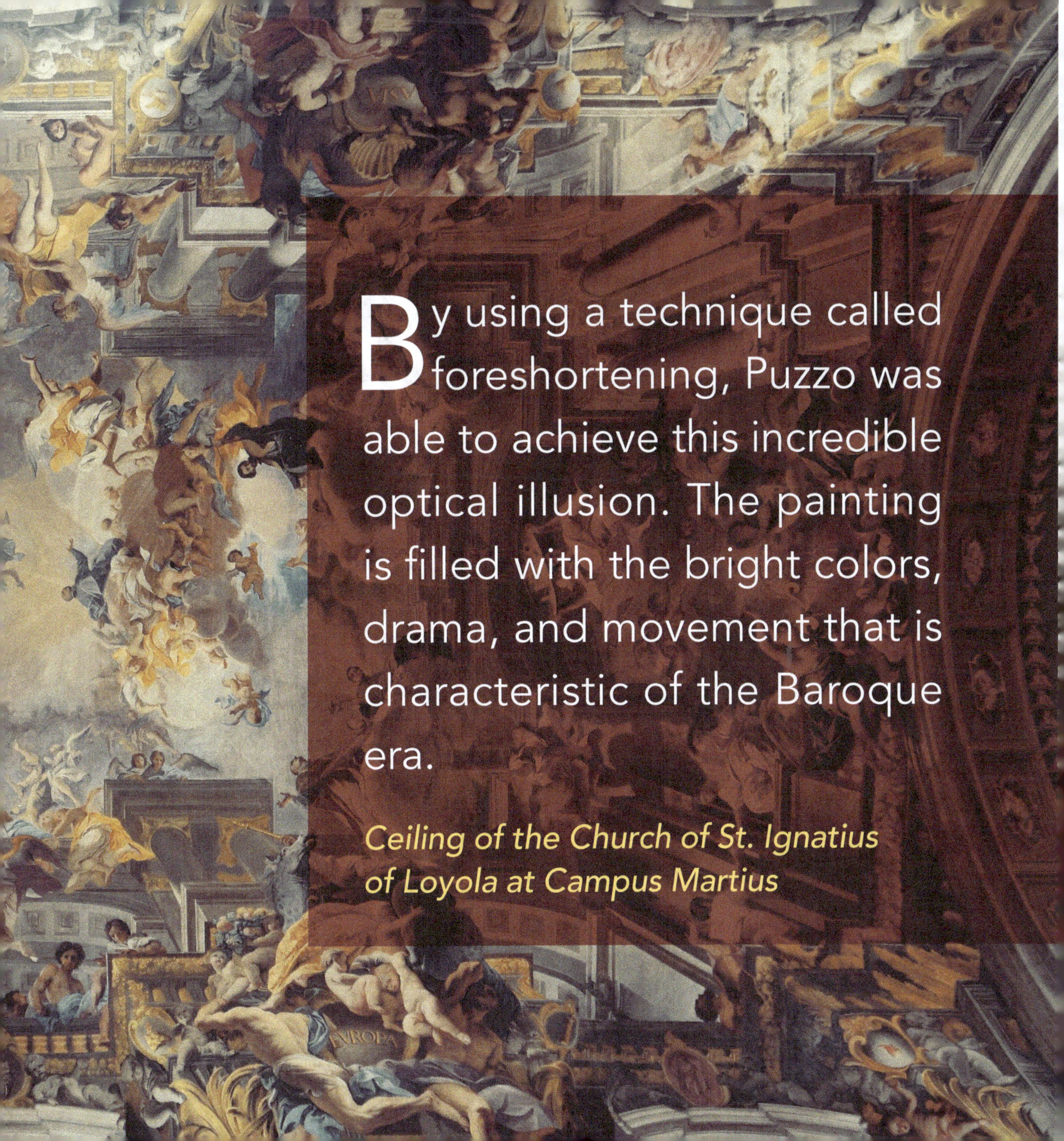

By using a technique called foreshortening, Puzzo was able to achieve this incredible optical illusion. The painting is filled with the bright colors, drama, and movement that is characteristic of the Baroque era.

Ceiling of the Church of St. Ignatius of Loyola at Campus Martius

Las Meninas
by Diego Velázquez

This amazing painting, painted in 1656 by Velazquez, is really a painting within a painting. At the left, the artist has painted himself with a huge canvas he's working on. We can't see the people that he's painting right away, but if you look at the back wall within the painting you will see that the king and queen are reflected in a mirror as they pose for him. The central figures are Margarita, who is a princess, and the **"maids of honor"** who surround her.

Las Meninas by Diego Velázquez

This is not a traditional portrait. Instead, it has the dramatic lighting and movement that is characteristic of the era. At the right, one of figures is playfully nudging a dog, and in the background we can see other paintings on the wall, as well as a figure going up the stairs. It's almost as if the artist was saying, "You expect me to complete this portrait with all this going on around me?"

Las Meninas (detail).

Awesome! Now you know more about Baroque Art and the artists who created it. You can find more Art, Music, & Photography books from Baby Professor by searching the website of your favorite book retailer.

Titus as a Monk by Rembrandt

Visit
BABY PROFESSOR
EDUCATION KIDS
www.BabyProfessorBooks.com
to download Free Baby Professor eBooks
and view our catalog of new and exciting
Children's Books